D1540801

CQ's Guide to the 2008 Elections

Gregory Giroux
Congressional Quarterly (CQ Politics.com)

CQ PRESS

A Division of Congressional Quarterly Inc.
Washington, D.C.

CQ Press
2300 N Street, NW, Suite 800
Washington, DC 20037

Phone: 202-729-1900; toll-free, 1-866-4CQ-PRESS (1-866-427-7737)

Web: www.cqpress.com

Copyright © 2008 by CQ Press, a division of Congressional Quarterly Inc.

Photo credits:
AP Images: front cover (all), 1, 4, 6, 11, 20 (Gravel), 21 (Vilsack), 22 (Giuliani), 24 (Paul), 25 (Romney), 26 (F. Thompson)
Scott J. Ferrell, *CQ Weekly:* 17, 18, 19, 20 (Kucinich, Obama), 21 (Richardson), 22 (Brownback, Gilmore), 23, 24 (McCain), 25 (Tancredo), 26 (T. Thompson)
Ben Relles: 33
Reuters: 14

Cover design: McGaughy Design
Composition: Auburn Associates, Inc.

(∞) The paper used in this publication exceeds the requirements of the American National Standard for Information Sciences—Permanence of Paper for Printed Library Materials, ANSI Z39.48-1992.

Printed and bound in the United States of America

11   10   09   08   07   1   2   3   4   5

ISBN 978-0-87289-777-9

Contents

Virginia Democrat Jim Webb (center) appears with supporters on November 9, 2006, after Republican senator George Allen conceded his loss to Webb two days after an election that clinched a majority of seats for Democrats in the U.S. Senate. Webb, who vigorously opposed the Iraq War, is brandishing a pair of combat boots that his son wore while serving in Iraq; he is pictured here with his wife, Hong Le Webb, and New York senator Charles E. Schumer, the chairman of the Democratic Senatorial Campaign Committee.

What's at Stake?

I see no good purpose being served by continuously and needlessly expending money and causing any more personal animosity."

In some form, those words have been spoken by numerous losing candidates for political office from whom we prefer graceful concession speeches over sore-loser demands to recount votes or contest an election outcome. Not until the closing months of the 2006 campaign, though, could anyone possibly have anticipated that those somber words of defeat would be uttered by Virginia Republican senator George Allen, whose loss to Democratic challenger Jim Webb was the Democrats' *coup de grâce* in one of the most cataclysmic and consequential elections in modern U.S. history.

Like so many of his Republican colleagues in Congress, Allen had initially been favored to win reelection in 2006 and help perpetuate Republican control of Congress. A former Virginia governor, Allen had generally been popular after defeating a Democratic senator in the 2000 election, and his mostly conservative Republican views seemed to dovetail with many voters in his home state, which has voted

Republican in each of the past ten presidential races. The Democrats initially struggled to recruit a strong candidate to oppose Allen.

But Allen was eventually swept out of office in a contest that was microcosmic of the Republican Party's struggles in the 2006 election, which saw the Democrats win control of both the U.S. House and the U.S. Senate in the final two years of the Republican administration of President George W. Bush. Allen's loss to Webb—by a mere 9,329 votes out of nearly 2.4 million cast—was the final Senate race that was called, and Allen's concession two days after the election guaranteed that the Democrats would control both houses of Congress when the 110th Congress convened in January 2007.

Dissatisfaction with the Bush administration and the Republican Party generally, and with the U.S. war in Iraq specifically, plus an especially aggressive and well-funded Democratic Party, contributed to Republican losses in Virginia and around the country. The Virginia race illustrated how much Bush was a drag on Republican candidates, even in districts and states that had voted just two years earlier to reelect him, sometimes by decisive margins. In 2004, Virginia backed Bush's reelection by 9 percentage points (54 percent to 45 percent of the votes) over Democratic nominee John Kerry. Yet by October 2006, Bush's approval rating in Virginia was just 39 percent, compared to a disapproval rating of 59 percent. This created an unfavorable political environment in which Allen was seeking reelection, and he and many of his Republican colleagues faced constant criticism that they were "rubber stamps" for an unpopular Bush administration.

The Virginia Senate race amply illustrated that campaigns and elections really do matter—and that one person's vote really does count. In a race as close as the Allen-Webb contest, one could pinpoint several factors that were decisive in determining the outcome. What if Allen had not committed some gaffes late in the campaign that allowed Webb to close the gap? Had Allen been able to squeeze another 9,330 votes out of the election—less than four votes per voting precinct—he would have won a second term and prevented Democrats from winning the Senate majority that has allowed them to dictate some of the policy agenda and thwart many of President Bush's domestic and foreign policy priorities.

Allen's loss also showed that politics in America are increasingly played on the margins, focused on a relatively small number of states and districts that are highly competitive and which can determine the balance of power of government. Most contests for the U.S. House and the U.S. Senate are so uncompetitive that they are virtually ignored by the national political parties, political action committees and interest groups who choose to focus their financial resources on a sliver of districts and states where there are close races.

Last but not least, the Virginia election demonstrated the importance of recruiting strong candidates for office. As a decorated veteran of the Vietnam War and a former Navy Secretary, Webb could speak with authority on U.S. policy in Iraq and on matters of national security that have long been an area of vulnerability for the Democratic Party. For decades, more voters have preferred the Republican Party to the Democratic Party on areas of national defense and foreign policy (while the Democratic Party has the edge over the Republican Party on domestic policy issues). In Webb, the Democrats had a candidate with strong credentials on national security issues (and who was formerly a Republican). Democratic leaders in Washington recognized Webb's strengths, and they took the highly unusual step of publicly supporting Webb in the Democratic primary election over another Democratic candidate. As the leading Senate Democratic campaign strategist wrote after the election, "Jim Webb fit like a glove."[1]

Story of the 2006 Midterm Elections

One day after the November 2006 mid-term congressional elections, President Bush described the outcome as a "thumpin'" for his Republican Party, which lost its majorities to the Democrats in both the U.S. House and Senate. That was almost certainly the first time any public figure, much less the president of the United States, employed that word to characterize the outcome of a national campaign. But "thumpin'" aptly described the devastating campaign season for Republicans that culminated in the Democrats claiming control of both chambers of Congress for the first time in a dozen years.

The 2006 congressional elections were the worst for Republicans since 1974, when the party suffered substantial losses in the elections that were held less than three months after President Richard M. Nixon resigned in the Watergate affair. All told, the Democrats made a net gain of 30 seats in the House, from controlling 203 of the 435 seats before the election to holding 233 seats when the 110th Congress convened in January 2007. The Democrats made a net gain of six seats in the Senate in the 2006 election, turning a 55–45 deficit to an operational majority of 51–49.

The Democrats' House victories also were historic in that they installed Rep. Nancy Pelosi of California as the first woman Speaker in American history. As House Speaker, Pelosi is the top-ranking official in the House of Representatives—and second in the presidential line of succession after the Vice President.

The Republicans suffered political losses across the board, from contests for the Senate and House to races for governor, state legislature, and mayoralties in cities large and small. In a sense, it was not terribly surprising that the Democrats made robust political gains in the 2006 election. More often than not, the political party that controls the White House sustains election losses in the midterm elections that are held between presidential election years (for example, 2006, 2002, 1998, etc.). The incumbent president's party usually suffers these losses at the halfway point of a presidential administration because the opposition party is more motivated to express displeasure with the White House than the incumbent party is to register support for the status quo.

Midterm election losses by the White House's party usually are more severe in the sixth year of a presidential administration—a phenomenon known as the "six year

Democratic leaders exult on November 7, 2006, after election returns pointed to big Democratic victories nationwide in races for the U.S. House and Senate. From left: Illinois representative Rahm Emanuel, the chairman of the Democratic Congressional Campaign Committee; House Minority Leader Nancy Pelosi of California, who became Speaker of the House; Senate Minority Leader Harry Reid of Nevada, who became Senate Majority Leader; and New York senator Charles E. Schumer, the chairman of the Democratic Senatorial Campaign Committee.

itch." In 1974, when Nixon resigned in the sixth year of his presidency, the Democrats made a net gain of 47 House seats. The 2006 election came at the end of the sixth year of Bush's presidency.

So why did the Democrats so thoroughly dominate elections in 2006? The most significant reason is that President Bush had poor approval ratings for most of the 2005–2006 campaign cycle. Democrats seized upon Bush's sagging numbers to brand numerous Republican incumbents and candidates as "rubber stamps" for the unpopular administration, while vowing to be agents of "change" in Washington.

According to the Gallup Poll, Bush's approval rating hovered around 50 percent in the first six months of 2005. It crept downward to about 40 percent in the second half of 2005, and then dipped to the mid-to-high 30s throughout 2006. The final Gallup Poll before the November 7 election pegged Bush's approval rating at 38 percent and his disapproval rating at 56 percent.

Bush's unpopularity was attributed mainly to widespread dissatisfaction with the U.S. war in Iraq, which in 2006 was entering its fourth year. A CNN "exit poll" of voters on Election Day 2006 found that 56 percent of respondents disapproved of the war—and they preferred Democratic congressional candidates to Republicans by a margin of 80 percent to 18 percent. An exit survey conducted by Democratic pollster Douglas E. Schoen found that a 22 percent plurality of voters identified the Iraq War as the most important issue in their vote for Congress—and 82 percent of those voters backed a Democrat. "I know there's a lot of speculation on what the election means for the battle we're waging in Iraq," President Bush said on November 8, 2006, the day after the election. "I recognize that many Americans voted last night to register their displeasure with the lack of progress being made there."

Voters also were skittish about the national economy and expressed concern about stagnating wages and the exploding costs of health care services and gasoline prices. As representatives of the incumbent party, the White House and congressional Republicans bore the brunt of the blame. Republican candidates also were hampered by a string of ethical or personal transgressions by some members of their party. This made it difficult for Republicans to publicize their achievements or share their policy prescriptions with voters:

- In July 2005, Rep. Don Sherwood, R.-Penn., acknowledged an affair with a young woman who had also accused the married congressman of physical abuse. Sherwood admitted to the affair but denied the abuse charges, and a lawsuit was settled

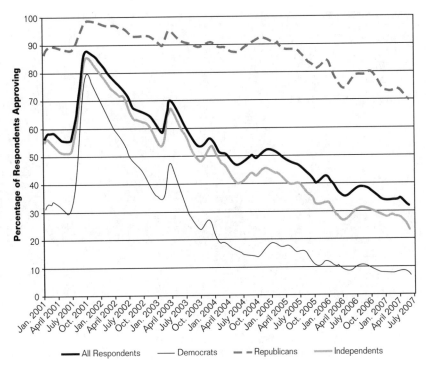

FIGURE 1
Approval of George W. Bush's Performance as President, 2001–2007

Source: Lowess-smoothed trends from 349 CBS News/*New York Times* and Gallup Polls.

out of court. Sherwood had been reelected to the House without Democratic opposition in both 2002 and 2004, but the affair and accusations of abuse contributed to his 2006 defeat to Democrat Christopher Carney.

- In December 2005, Rep. Duke Cunningham, R.-Calif., resigned from Congress after admitting to taking large bribes from defense contractors.
- In June 2006, Rep. Tom DeLay, R.-Texas, who was the House Majority Leader at the beginning of the 109th Congress (2005–2006), resigned from Congress rather than wage a reelection bid that would have been very difficult to win as a result of DeLay's indictment on campaign finance charges in Texas. DeLay denied wrongdoing, but he was too politically weakened to remain in Congress.
- In September 2006, less than two months before the election, Rep. Bob Ney, R.-Ohio, pleaded guilty to federal corruption charges that stemmed from an investigation into his ties to former lobbyist Jack Abramoff. Ney's decision to resign just a few days before the election delivered a *coup de grâce* to his own Republican Party, which badly lost the election in Ney's district.
- Also in September 2006, it was revealed that Rep. Mark Foley, R.-Fla., had sent inappropriate electronic messages to several young male pages who perform administrative functions for the House of Representatives. Foley resigned from

In the 2006 election, some Republican lawmakers were hampered by their ties to Jack Abramoff (left), a well-connected Republican lobbyist who pleaded guilty in January 2006 to conspiracy, mail fraud, and tax evasion.

Congress on September 29, less than six weeks before the election, and his Republican-leaning district in south Florida was captured by Democratic businessman Tim Mahoney.

Democrats regularly claimed that such wrongdoing by Republican members of Congress created a "culture of corruption" in Washington. Democratic leaders promised on the campaign trail to run the most ethical Congress in history if they were returned to the majority. Republican strategists acknowledged that questions about the ethical behavior of some of their members created significant political liabilities in the 2006 elections. Sherwood, DeLay, Cunningham, Ney, and Foley all represented Republican-leaning districts and probably would have been easily reelected in 2006 absent any actual or alleged wrongdoing. Instead, Democrats were elected to the Sherwood, DeLay, Ney, and Foley seats and very nearly won Cunningham's seat.

"We also lost several seats by self-inflicted wounds," New York representative Thomas M. Reynolds, the chairman of the National Republican Congressional Committee (NRCC), said after the election. "We had a number of reliable Republican seats where the member had a problem. And either they could not straighten it out with their constituents, or they left it to the candidate succeeding them to deal with it."

Some Republicans argued that during the Bush presidency their party did not adhere to its fiscally conservative principles of reducing government and cutting federal spending and budget deficits. Therefore, they deserved to lose because they failed to practice what they preached. Alan Greenspan, the former chairman of the Federal Reserve, wrote in a 2007 memoir that, "Republicans in Congress lost their way. They swapped principle for power. They ended up with neither. They deserved to lose."[2] "We didn't lose the 2006 election because of the war in Iraq," Arizona senator John McCain, a contender for the 2008 Republican presidential nomination, said during a Republican presidential debate in May 2007. "We lost it because we in the Republican Party came to Washington to change government, and government changed us. We let spending go out of control. We spent money like a drunken sailor."[3]

All of these factors created an ideal political environment for the opposition Democratic Party, which parlayed the Republicans' struggles into raising robust campaign funds and recruiting top-flight Democratic candidates to oppose Republican lawmakers who were politically vulnerable. Two top Democrats who were instrumental in raising money and recruiting candidates were Illinois representative Rahm Emanuel and New York senator Charles E. Schumer, who headed the House and Senate Democratic campaign organizations respectively.

House Contests: A Real Thumpin'

When election day arrived, it seemed certain that the Democrats would gain at least the fifteen House seats that they needed to win control of the House. They would win thirty seats—exactly twice as many as the Democrats needed to control the House.

Early on election night, the Democrats scored big triumphs in Kentucky and Indiana, the two states where most polling stations close at 6:00 p.m. eastern time— earlier than in other states. In Kentucky's Louisville-centered 3rd District, the upset of five-term Republican representative Anne M. Northup by Democrat John A. Yarmuth, a newspaper publisher, seemed to presage big Democratic gains elsewhere in the nation. So too did the losses of three Republican incumbents in Indiana: Chris Chocola, who lost his bid for a second term to lawyer Joe Donnelly in the northern 2nd District; John Hostettler, who was trounced by Brad Ellsworth, a county sheriff in Evansville, in the southwestern 8th District; and Mike Sodrel, who was defeated by Democratic former representative Baron Hill in their third consecutive match-up in the southeastern 9th District, where Hill had been reelected in 2002 but lost in 2004. The biggest Democratic gains came in Pennsylvania, where the Democrats defeated four Republican incumbents and nearly defeated a fifth. (The Democratic wins in Pennsylvania were a painful irony for the Pennsylvania Republican state legislators who had just a few years earlier redrawn the state's congressional district map to their partisan advantage—or so they thought).

In mid-December, Democrats increased their overall House gains in the 2006 election to an even thirty seats when Democratic former Rep. Ciro D. Rodriguez defeated Republican Rep. Henry Bonilla in a runoff election in Texas' 23rd District in and around San Antonio. The unusual December election was held because the Supreme Court in June had invalidated Bonilla's district on the grounds that its 55 percent Hispanic population percentage was insufficient to satisfy federal Voting Rights Act protections for racial and ethic minorities to elect candidates of choice. As redrawn that August by a federal court, the 23rd District now had a 65 percent Hispanic population and a more pronounced Democratic lean. Rodriguez's victory over Bonilla was icing on the cake for Democrats.

No House Democratic incumbent was defeated, and Democrats also won every district that members of their party had left open to retire or seek other political office. Few House Democratic incumbents faced close races. Just five were reelected by less than 10 percentage points: John Barrow of Georgia's 12th District (won by 0.6 percentage points); Jim Marshall of Georgia's 8th District (1.1 percentage points); Leonard L. Boswell of Iowa's 3rd District (5.2 percentage points); Melissa Bean of Illinois' 8th District (6.9 percentage points); and Julia Carson of Indiana's 7th District (7.5 percentage points).

In sum, Democratic candidates for the House received 42.2 million votes nationwide, or 53 percent of the total. Republican candidates for the House received 35.7 million votes, or 45 percent of the total. Independent and third-party candidates received 2.5 million votes, or 2 percent of the total.[4]

Senate Contests: Just by a Margin

The Democratic capture of the U.S. Senate in the 2006 election seemingly was more improbable than the party's winning a majority of House seats—but no less impressive. That the Democrats would win control of the Senate seemed unthinkable. The 2004 election had demoralized Democrats and emboldened Republicans, who made a net gain of four Senate seats to extend their majority over the Democrats to 55–45. In the thirty-three Senate races that would be contested in 2006, the Republicans were

TABLE 1 House Seats that Flipped from Republican to Democratic Control

STATE (DISTRICT)	REPUBLICAN LOSER	DEMOCRATIC WINNER
Arizona (5)	J.D. Hayworth[a]	Harry E. Mitchell
Arizona (8)	Randy Graf[b]	Gabrielle Giffords
California (11)	Richard Pombo[a]	Jerry McNerney
Colorado (7)	Rick O'Donnell[b]	Ed Perlmutter
Connecticut (2)	Rob Simmons[a]	Joe Courtney
Connecticut (5)	Nancy Johnson[a]	Christopher S. Murphy
Florida (16)	Joe Negron[b]	Tim Mahoney
Florida (22)	E. Clay Shaw[a]	Ron Klein
Indiana (2)	Chris Chocola[a]	Joe Donnelly
Indiana (8)	John Hostettler[a]	Brad Ellsworth
Indiana (9)	Mike Sodrel[a]	Baron P. Hill
Iowa (1)	Mike Whalen[b]	Bruce Braley
Iowa (2)	Jim Leach[a]	David Loebsack
Kansas (2)	Jim Ryun[a]	Nancy Boyda
Kentucky (3)	Anne Northup[a]	John Yarmuth
Minnesota (1)	Gil Gutknecht[a]	Tim Walz
New Hampshire (1)	Jeb Bradley[a]	Carol Shea-Porter
New Hampshire (2)	Charles Bass[a]	Paul W. Hodes
New York (19)	Sue Kelly[a]	John Hall
New York (20)	John E. Sweeney[a]	Kirsten Gillibrand
New York (24)	Ray Meier[b]	Michael Arcuri
North Carolina (11)	Charles H. Taylor[a]	Heath Shuler
Ohio (18)	Joy Padgett[b]	Zack Space
Pennsylvania (4)	Melissa Hart[a]	Jason Altmire
Pennsylvania (7)	Curt Weldon[a]	Joe Sestak
Pennsylvania (8)	Mike Fitzpatrick[a]	Patrick Murphy
Pennsylvania (10)	Dan Sherwood[a]	Christopher Carney
Texas (22)	Shelley Sekula-Gibbs[b]	Nick Lampson
Texas (23)	Henry Bonilla[a]	Ciro D. Rodriguez
Wisconsin (8)	John Gard[b]	Steve Kagen

[a] Incumbent
[b] Open seat

Source: Adapted from http://en.wikipedia.org/wiki/United_States_House_elections,_2006.

the defending party in just fifteen states and the Democrats were the defending party in eighteen states. Therefore, in order for the Democrats to garner the fifty-one Senate seats they needed to win a majority, they would have to make a net gain of six Senate seats in the 2006 election—a tall order of winning every state in which they were the defending party and capturing six of the states where the Republicans were the incumbent party. It is very rare for a political party to make a net gain of six Senate seats in an election year.

Democratic leaders recognized their long odds: Nevada senator Harry Reid, the Democratic leader in the Senate, said on the Senate floor in April 2005 that it would take a "little miracle" for Democrats to realize the gains that would install them as the majority party after the 2006 elections. With Vice President Dick Cheney available to break any 50–50 ties in the Republicans' favor, the GOP could afford to lose five Senate seats in the 2006 election and still retain majority control of the Senate. They could not afford to lose six seats. Never before in the history of the direct election of U.S. senators (established in 1913 by the Seventeenth Amendment) has a political party made a net gain of six Senate seats when it had more seats to defend than the other party.

The Democrats achieved this historical first by defeating Republican incumbents in Missouri, Montana, Ohio, Pennsylvania, Rhode Island, and Virginia; reelecting all of their incumbents who sought reelection; and defending three states that Democratic senators had left open to retire.[5] The only Republican who was first elected to the Senate in 2006 was Bob Corker of Tennessee, a former Chattanooga mayor who narrowly defeated Democratic representative Harold E. Ford Jr. for the seat of retiring Senate Majority Leader Bill Frist.

The Senate Democrats' campaigns were greatly aided by the fundraising heft of the Democratic Senatorial Campaign Committee (DSCC), which is the political organization that is responsible for heading up the party's fundraising, candidate recruitment, and overall strategy for Senate races. Headed by New York Sen. Charles E. Schumer, who is one of the Democratic Party's most potent fundraisers, the DSCC in the 2005–2006 campaign cycle raised $121.4 million, or a 37 percent increase above the $88.7 million that it raised in the 2003–2004 campaign cycle. The DSCC's partisan counterpart, the National Republican Senatorial Committee (NRSC), reported raising $88.8 million in the 2005–2006 campaign cycle, or 12 percent above the $79 million it raised in the 2003–2004 campaign cycle. So the DSCC outraised the NRSC by more than $30 million in the 2005–2006 campaign cycle.[6]

Throughout the 2005–2006 campaign cycle, the DSCC had a robust advantage in available cash on hand because it generally spent a smaller share of its overall campaign receipts than the NRSC. The fundraising edge enabled the DSCC to air television commercials to boost their preferred candidates and attack their opponents much more vigorously than the NRSC could defend its candidates in the waning weeks and months of the 2006 campaign.

One common thread of the Democratic Senate campaign was its fielding of first-rate Democratic challengers who had a history of running statewide elections and who were ready for the rough-and-tumble of a Senate campaign. The DSCC aggressively pursued candidates it thought had the best chance of winning in 2006, and in

New York senator Charles E. Schumer (left), the chairman of the Democratic Senatorial Campaign Committee, appears with Rhode Island Democrat Sheldon Whitehouse, a former state attorney general whose defeat of Republican senator Lincoln Chafee helped Democrats clinch a majority of Senate seats in the 2006 election.

nearly every case the DSCC was successful. In Pennsylvania, Democratic officials persuaded state treasurer Bob Casey to challenge Republican senator Rick Santorum; Casey was the son of a popular former governor and a prodigious vote-getter in his own right, having won a landslide victory as Pennsylvania treasurer in the November 2004 election. While some liberal Democratic activists bristled at some of Casey's positions, the recruitment effort by the national Democratic Party ensured that Casey would not be seriously challenged in the Democratic primary election. This was a sharp departure from the Democratic campaign against Santorum in 2000, when there was no top-flight Democratic candidate in a crowded primary election and the party's eventual nominee was not as well-known or as well-funded as Casey would be in 2006. Schumer later wrote that "aggressive candidate selection—through both recruitment and intervention in primaries—contributed to winning the Senate majority more than any other (even more than our fundraising advantage, which was significant, to be sure)."[7]

The Democratic Senate victories also were aided by the Republicans' failure to recruit strong challengers to many Democratic incumbents, for whom competitive races never materialized. In North Dakota, popular Republican governor John Hoeven declined to challenge Democratic senator Kent Conrad in a state that usually votes strongly Republican in presidential races; President Bush won 60 percent of the vote in North Dakota in the 2004 presidential campaign. But Republicans did not field a strong candidate against Conrad, who won 69 percent of the vote. In Florida, where Democratic senator Bill Nelson was seeking a second term in a politically competitive state, the Republican nominee was Rep. Katherine Harris, the former Florida Secretary of State whose controversial role in the 2000 presidential recount in that state rendered her a flawed candidate. The significant staff turnover on Harris' campaign accentuated her struggles, and Harris lost to Nelson by more than 20 percentage points.

The following summaries describe how the Democrats made the net gain of six seats that enabled them to clinch a majority of Senate seats in the 2006 election.

Missouri (Democratic state auditor Claire McCaskill unseated Republican senator Jim Talent, 49.6 percent to 47.3 percent).

Missouri has long been viewed as a closely divided "bellwether" state that is nearly evenly divided between the two parties and which is an unusually good barometer of national political trends. In only one presidential election in the twentieth century (1956) did Missouri not vote for the national winner.

The early part of this decade saw Republicans take a bit of an edge, with President Bush having carried the state in 2004 by 7 percentage points and Jim Talent having defeated appointed Democratic senator Jean Carnahan two years earlier in a special election. But Bush's declining popularity in Missouri hurt Republican incumbent Talent and boosted Democratic challenger McCaskill, who won the Senate race just two years after she narrowly lost the state's race for governor to Republican Matt Blunt. McCaskill performed well among the state's suburban voters near Kansas City and St. Louis. But this time she also did better in the state's normally Republican-leaning rural constituencies than she had in her 2004 loss to Blunt.

Montana (Democrat Jon Tester, the president of the Montana Senate, defeated three-term Republican senator Conrad Burns, 49.2 percent to 48.3 percent).

Like other Republican incumbents on the ballot in 2006, Burns was burdened by the strong anti-Republican political environment that prevailed nationally. But some of Burns' problems were self-inflicted: he took $150,000 campaign contributions from the disgraced lobbyist Jack Abramoff (or from Abramoff's firm or his clients). That enabled Tester to argue that the senator had grown too close to lobbyists and moneyed interests after nearly two decades in Washington. Burns also committed some gaffes, perhaps the most damaging was when he berated a group of firefighters for doing a "piss-poor job" fighting a fire in eastern Montana. Tester prevailed by nine-tenths of one percentage point—the second-closest Senate race of the 2006 election in terms of percentage point margin.

Ohio (Democratic representative Sherrod Brown defeated two-term Republican senator Mike DeWine, 56 percent to 44 percent).

The 2006 campaign year was a difficult one for Ohio Republicans, whose dominance of Ohio elections for the past dozen years meant that they would bear the brunt of the blame from voters who were disgusted with how the state was being run. It didn't help DeWine that Ohio Republican governor Bob Taft was convicted in August 2005 of misdemeanor campaign finance violations, or that Ohio Republican representative Bob Ney pleaded guilty in September 2006 to federal corruption charges.

DeWine also had a formidable opponent in Brown, a well-funded challenger who ran as an unapologetic liberal opposed to the Iraq war. Brown also denounced trade pacts that he claimed had led to stagnating wages at home and an "outsourcing" of jobs overseas. DeWine tried to paint Brown as too politically liberal on tax and national security issues, but his attempts to seriously wound Brown were unsuccessful. Brown's liberal views might have been a liability in a different election year, but he coasted down the stretch and defeated DeWine by 12 percentage points.

Pennsylvania (Democratic state treasurer Bob Casey defeated two-term Republican senator Rick Santorum, 59 percent to 41 percent).

No Republican senator up for reelection in 2006 began the election year in a more politically precarious position than Santorum, a staunch conservative in a state that has usually voted Democratic—including in each of the past four presidential elections. Casey decided to enter the race early in 2005 after heavy recruiting from Democratic leaders in Washington and Pennsylvania. Casey was the preferred candidate because he had widespread name recognition throughout the state as a result of winning statewide elections in Pennsylvania—Casey was elected state auditor in 1996 and 2000 and elected state treasurer in 2004—and because he was the namesake son of a popular late governor.

Some liberal groups bristled at the Democratic Party's courting of Casey because they did not like Casey's opposition to abortion rights and gun control measures. But their dislike of Santorum was far stronger, and the strong anti-Republican political environment made it difficult for Santorum to gain traction. Casey held a solid lead in public opinion polls from start to finish, and he won by 18 percentage points in what was the most lopsided defeat for an incumbent U.S. senator in the 2006 election.

Rhode Island (Democrat Sheldon Whitehouse, a former state attorney general, defeated one-term Republican senator Lincoln Chafee, 54 percent to 46 percent).

At first glance, it would seem hardly shocking that the Democrats would prevail in a Senate race in Rhode Island, which is probably the most Democratic-leaning state in the nation. But in the 2006 campaign, Chafee, a popular liberal Republican who had easily won a full six-year term in 2000, was seeking reelection. Lincoln Chafee's reelection bid was, however, complicated by the candidacy of Republican primary challenger Stephen Laffey, a conservative mayor of Cranston who criticized Chafee's moderate voting record. Chafee won the primary by 54 percent to 46 percent—ironically, with campaign help from Republican officials with whom Chafee did not always see eye-to-eye but who believed that Chafee was a more electable Republican than Laffey in Democratic-leaning Rhode Island.

In the general election, Chafee was hampered by President Bush's abysmal approval rating, which at one point sank to 22 percent in Rhode Island. Whitehouse concentrated more on attacking the Bush administration and Republicans in general than on Chafee's record, and Whitehouse's call for a pullout of U.S. troops from Iraq resonated with voters.

Virginia (Democrat Jim Webb, an author and former Navy secretary, unseated Republican senator George Allen, 49.6 percent to 49.2 percent).

Webb's unlikely victory over Allen clinched a fifty-first seat in the 110th Congress—and a Senate majority—for the Democrats. As the 2006 campaign year began, political analysts were speculating about Allen's race—for the White House in 2008. Allen's reelection to the Senate in 2006 seemed assured, particularly after popular Democratic governor Mark Warner said in 2005 that he would not challenge the senator.

Webb initially did not appear to pose a serious threat to Allen's reelection campaign. Webb entered the Senate race only in February 2006, just four months before a June primary election that already included Harris Miller, a technology association executive and Democratic activist. And some Democratic voters were skeptical of Webb, a first-time candidate for elected political office who had been a Republican for most of his adult life. But other Democrats liked Webb, who split from the Republican Party over economic issues and also his opposition to the Iraq war, which Webb opposed from the start. Party officials saw the former Navy secretary and Vietnam War veteran as someone who could help the Democratic Party go toe-to-toe with the Republicans on national security issues. The DSCC endorsed Webb shortly before the June primary election, which Webb won by 7 percentage points.

Webb gained his footing as a campaigner in the summer and fall, though he probably would not have edged out Allen without help from a series of mainly self-inflicted political wounds the incumbent suffered. At one campaign event, Allen ridiculed an Indian-American Webb supporter by calling him a "macaca;" the senator claimed he did not know that the word is a racial epithet that refers to a monkey, but the damage was done. Allen lost overwhelmingly to Webb in liberal-leaning college and university towns and in the northern Virginia suburbs. Two days after the election, Allen conceded to Webb, whose victory by four-tenths of one percentage point was the closest Senate race of 2006.

Virginia Republican Sen. George Allen's loss to Democratic challenger Jim Webb in 2006 ended Allen's Senate career after one term and also extinguished any ambitions he had for the presidency in 2008. Several factors contributed to Allen's loss to Webb, including an unfavorable political environment for Republicans and campaign gaffes such as Allen's reference to an Indian-American volunteer for Webb as a "macaca."

Gubernatorial Races and State Legislative Races

Democrats also made robust gains in the thirty-six governor's races that were on the ballot in 2006, winning six governorships that had been held by the Republicans. As of 2007, there were twenty-eight Democratic governors and twenty-two Republican governors—a mirror image of the partisan composition of the nation's governors that prevailed before the 2006 election.

In Maryland, Republican governor Robert L. Ehrlich Jr. was defeated by Democratic challenger Martin O'Malley, the mayor of Baltimore. In five other contests the retiring Republican governor was replaced with a Democrat: Arkansas, where state attorney general Mike Beebe was elected to succeed Mike Huckabee; Colorado, where former Denver district attorney Bill Ritter succeeded Bill Owens; Massachusetts, where lawyer Deval Patrick succeeded Mitt Romney; New York, where state attorney general Eliot Spitzer succeeded George E. Pataki; and Ohio, where Democratic representative Ted Strickland succeeded Bob Taft.

State legislative contests in 2006 also felt the national Democratic wave. Of the eleven state legislative chambers that saw a shift in party control, the Democrats gained control from the Republicans in all but one instance. Some of the most astounding Democratic gains came in New Hampshire, where the Democrats had a net gain of more than 90 seats in the state House, which with 400 members is the largest state legislative body in the nation. In the swing state of Minnesota, a net Democratic gain of 19 seats in the state House was more than sufficient to erase the Republicans' razor-thin 68–66 majority in that chamber.

The Democratic gains were attributed mainly to the poor political environment for Republicans nationally, and they were in keeping with recent historical trends that point to large losses in congressional and state legislative contests in midterm election years for the party that controls the White House. In 1994, when Republicans made huge gains nationally to win control of the U.S. House and Senate, they also made substantial gains in state legislative contests.

Political Geography of the 2006 Elections

The Democratic victories in the 2006 elections were fairly uniform throughout the country, but the returns confirmed some enduring characteristics about each party's strengths and weaknesses in specific regions.

The 2006 elections intensified the strongly Democratic leanings of New England, a six-state region in the northeastern United States where the active two-party competition included a vibrant liberal wing of the Republican Party that was personified by politicians such as Nelson Rockefeller, the former New York governor and vice president. But New England has since become a Democratic bastion, and the region fortified its Democratic proclivities in the 2006 election. New England is heavily Catholic and is generally closely aligned with labor unions—two demographics that have for years been more closely identified with the Democratic Party than with the Republican Party. The region also includes a burgeoning population of young urban professionals who are more liberal than conservative and a small number of religious conservative voters who tend to vote Republican.

In New Hampshire, Democratic challengers unseated both Republican congressmen, making the 110th Congress (2007–2008) the first in nearly a century to feature an all-Democratic U.S. House delegation in New Hampshire. Two of the three Connecticut Republicans in the U.S. House were defeated—and the third, Christopher Shays, barely retained his seat. When the 110th Congress convened in January 2007, Shays was the only Republican in the House from New England.

The Democrats made marginal gains in the South in the 2006 election, though the Republicans emerged with a more dominant advantage there than in any other major region. Even after the Republicans' debacle, the party still held 85 of the 142 House seats and 21 of the 26 Senate seats in the thirteen states that Congressional Quarterly considers as Southern: Alabama; Arkansas; Florida; Georgia; Kentucky; Louisiana; Mississippi; North Carolina; Oklahoma; South Carolina; Tennessee; Texas; and Virginia. The Republicans have done well in the South mainly because the region includes a sizable population of Protestants, including many evangelical conservatives. Labor unions also are not as strong in the South as they are in the North.

In the industrial Midwest—states like Illinois, Michigan, Ohio and Pennsylvania— the Democrats made some major inroads in the 2006 election. By and large, this region is skittish about international trade pacts that detractors say "outsource" U.S. jobs to other countries that have much lower labor costs. Some of the most impressive Democratic victories in the 2006 election came in Pennsylvania, where the Democratic governor was overwhelmingly reelected, a Republican senator was trounced for reelection and four Republican members of the U.S. House were defeated.

The Democrats continue to perform well in the Pacific Coast states of California, Washington, and Oregon, where five of the six U.S. senators and forty-four of the sixty-seven U.S. House members in the 110th Congress are Democrats. All three states include many culturally liberal residents, and Democratic-leaning Hispanics comprise about one-third of all residents in California, by far the nation's most populous state. Notwithstanding the political success of California Republican governor Arnold Schwarzenegger, a moderate Republican, the Pacific Coast is more likely to stay Democratic-leaning for years to come.

The 2006 election indicated that the Mountain West will be a key swing constituency. While this region has historically leaned Republican, it is witnessing burgeoning population growth that has made the area more politically independent than Republican-leaning or Democratic-leaning. One key 2008 contest that could lend insights about the political leanings of the Mountain West is the Senate race in Colorado. The contestants will be Representative Mark Udall, a mainly liberal Democrat, and former representative Bob Schaffer, a mostly conservative Republican. Both men will be courting the state's large bloc of independent-minded voters.

2008 Presidential Race

No sooner had the last votes of the 2006 election been counted than prospective candidates for president in 2008 began preparing their campaigns for the White House. Presidential hopefuls began actively raising money and building campaign organizations early in 2007. The 2008 presidential race is the most wide-open contest for the White House in decades. Not since 1928 did a presidential election not include an incumbent president or vice president seeking the White House. President Bush is barred by the Twenty-second Amendment to the U.S. Constitution from running again in 2008, and Vice President Dick Cheney confirmed after the 2004 election that he would not be a candidate for president.

Nearly twenty serious Democrats and Republicans were seeking the presidency at some point in 2007. But some notable politicians declined to run. They included Tennessee Democrat Al Gore, the former vice president and senator who narrowly lost the 2000 presidential race to Bush; Democrat Mark Warner, the former Virginia governor who later decided to run for the Senate; Georgia Republican Newt Gingrich, the former House Speaker; and Tennessee Republican Bill Frist, the former Senate majority leader.

But Democratic and Republican voters have plenty of candidates to choose from in the 2008 presidential election. Each major Democratic and Republican presidential candidate is briefly profiled below. (The capsule descriptions appear in alphabetical order by last name, beginning with the Democrats.)

Democratic Candidates

Joseph R. Biden Jr.
Senator
Delaware

No candidate in either field has served in Congress longer than Biden, who was first elected to the Senate in 1972 and who won a sixth six-year term in 2002. And no candidate has boasted stronger foreign policy credentials than the Delaware senator, who in the 110th Congress (2007–2008) served as chairman of the Senate Foreign Relations Committee.

Biden has been a vocal critic of the Bush administration's policies in Iraq and has promoted a plan to quell sectarian violence there by essentially dividing the nation into autonomous Shiite, Sunni, and Kurdish regions while maintaining a central government to secure the nation's borders and distribute oil revenues, While he has criticized the Bush administration's policies in Iraq, Biden has chided some of his Democratic presidential contenders for supporting troop withdrawal plans that Biden said were unworkable. In 2007, Biden called on his Democratic competitors to join him in a debate devoted exclusively to the war in Iraq.

Biden lagged far behind other better-known competitors in fundraising and in early polls, which led some detractors to speculate in 2007 that Biden could not win the race and was instead effectively auditioning to become Secretary of State in a Democratic presidential administration. But Biden has dismissed early poll numbers as meaningless and has said they were not reflective of what he was hearing from supporters in early primary states.

Biden's 2008 White House campaign is his second bid for the presidency. He also sought the Democratic nomination in 1988, but was forced to withdraw in September 1987 after he was dogged by accusations of plagiarism.

Hillary Rodham Clinton
Senator
New York

Clinton announced her presidential candidacy in January 2007 to the surprise of no one, and she quickly became the undisputed front-runner in the Democratic field. Clinton, who transitioned from First Lady to senator following the 2000 election, has a deep reservoir of political support and is backed by many Democratic women who would like to see Clinton become the country's first woman president. Throughout 2007, Clinton raised tens of millions of dollars and built a formidable campaign organization that drew the top staff talent in national Democratic circles. In the summer of 2007, it seemed highly likely that she would be the Democratic presidential nominee.

Clinton's biggest obstacle to winning the presidency is that she is a deeply polarizing figure, with adoring supporters who are as committed to supporting her candidacy as are the legions of critics who are prepared to vote against her. Throughout 2007, polls showed that Clinton had universal name recognition and that nearly as many voters disapproved as approved of her. Some Republicans strategists prefer that the Democrats nominate Clinton, on the grounds that she is so polarizing that her candidacy would rally Republican voters to the polls. But other Republican strategists recognize that Clinton is a smart politician and a formidable candidate who should not be underestimated.

Clinton has taken some flak throughout her presidential campaign from some liberal activists who criticized her vote in 2002 to authorize war in Iraq, as well as her refusal to later repudiate that vote as a mistake. The criticism has not deeply wounded Clinton's candidacy, though, and she has said she is committed to ending the war in Iraq.

Christopher Dodd
Senator
Connecticut

Among the most politically experienced presidential contenders in either party. Dodd was elected to the U.S. House in 1974 at age 30, and six years later won his first of five Senate terms. In the 110th Congress (2007–2008), Dodd served as chairman of the Senate Banking, Housing and Urban Affairs Committee.

In August 2007 Dodd received the endorsement of the International Association of Fire Fighters (IAFF), which in 2004 backed the successful Democratic presidential primary campaign of Massachusetts senator John Kerry.

Like most of the major Democratic contenders, Dodd backed the 2002 Iraq war resolution. But Dodd moved in 2007 to distinguish himself from his Democratic rivals—particularly New York senator Hillary Rodham Clinton and Illinois senator Barack Obama—on Iraq policy. Dodd has repeatedly stated that any congressional legislation pertaining to Iraq needed to establish firm deadlines for a complete withdrawal of U.S. troops from that nation. "I urge Senators Obama and Clinton not to backtrack on the need for a firm, enforceable deadline and state clearly and directly whether they will support an Iraq measure if it does not include one," Dodd said in September 2007.

John Edwards
Former Senator
North Carolina

Four years after he sought the Democratic presidential nomination and wound up as his party's vice-presidential nominee, Edwards made a second bid for the Democratic presidential nomination in 2008 with a focus on curbing poverty and making sure that economic growth percolates to lower-income earners. Edwards announced his presidential candidacy on December 28, 2006 in New Orleans, in the city's Lower Ninth Ward, which had been decimated sixteen months earlier by Hurricane Katrina and continued to recover.

Edwards was a successful trial lawyer before embarking on his political career, and his 2008 presidential campaign had early success raising money largely because of political contributions from fellow attorneys. In early 2007, Edwards also polled well in Iowa, where his second-place showing in the 2004 kickoff presidential caucuses helped establish Edwards as the chief competitor to Massachusetts senator John Kerry (who won the Democratic nomination and later chose Edwards as his running mate). Yet Edwards' second presidential campaign in 2008 has faced difficult competition from Hillary Rodham Clinton and Barack Obama.

Mike Gravel
Former Senator
Alaska

Gravel entered the 2008 Democratic presidential race as the most militantly anti-war candidate—and also the longest of long shots. Gravel, who turned 77 in May 2007, last ran for political office in 1980, when he sought a third Senate term and lost in the Democratic primary. Gravel has said repeatedly that no Democratic presidential candidate who voted to authorize war in Iraq in 2002 is qualified to serve as president. He has raised little money for his presidential campaign.

Dennis J. Kucinich
Congressman
Ohio

Kucinich, who has represented Cleveland in the U.S. House since 1997, waged a bid for the Democratic presidential nomination in 2004 that was motivated by his opposition to the Iraq war. He again emphasized anti-war themes in his second bid for the presidency in 2008. Kucinich's anti-war views predate the Iraq war. Kucinich has promoted a federal Department of Peace to resolve conflicts. On September 10, 2007, Kucinich was the only member of the House of Representatives who voted "no" on a resolution to commemorate the sixth anniversary of the September 11, 2001, terrorist attacks. Kucinich said that he supported the victims and honored the memories of those who were killed in the terrorist attacks, but said he would not support the resolution because the Bush administration "launched a war against Iraq, conflating the true tragedy of September 11 with lies about weapons of mass destruction." [8] On other issues, Kucinich supports a "single payer" government-run health care system as the best vehicle for providing universal health care services.

Barack Obama
Senator
Illinois

After initially rejecting a 2008 presidential campaign, Obama changed course and announced his candidacy in February 2007. Obama became a political celebrity following a well-received speech to the 2004 Democratic national convention in Boston that made him a household name in Democratic circles even before he was elected to the Senate that November. Just 46 years old at the beginning of 2008, Obama projects a youthfulness and idealism that drew comparisons to former New York senator Robert F. Kennedy, who competed for the Democratic presidential nomination in 1968 prior to his assassination in June of that year. Obama had phenomenal success raising campaign funds in 2007; through the first six months of that year, Obama had more individual campaign donors than any candidate in either party.

Obama's detractors decry his lack of national experience, noting that he was elected to the Senate just in 2004. Obama, who previously served in the Illinois Senate, sought to turn his sparse Washington experience into a positive by portraying himself as an "outsider" at a time when many Americans harbor unfavorable feelings toward Congress and the White House. "I may not have the experience Washington likes," Obama said in September 2007, "but I believe I have the experience America needs right now."[9]

Obama was not in the Senate in 2002, when his major Democratic opponents voted for the resolution that authorized the Bush administration to wage military operations in Iraq. Obama has said that he opposed the war from the start, and in September 2007 he called for withdrawing all U.S. troops from Iraq by the end of 2008.

Bill Richardson
Governor
New Mexico

Richardson wields one of the most eclectic political resumes of any White House hopeful: more than fourteen years in the U.S. House; one year as U.S. ambassador to the United Nations; three years as energy secretary to President Bill Clinton; and five years as governor of New Mexico. Richardson's political assets include his Hispanic ethnicity, which could be a plus in courting votes from that politically influential and Democratic-leaning voting bloc; his political base in the Mountain West, a fast-growing and politically independent region; and his tenure as a state governor, the political stepping-stone of four of the past five presidents, including Bill Clinton and George W. Bush.

In the summer of 2007, Richardson was usually in fourth place in Democratic presidential preference surveys—behind Clinton, Obama, and Edwards, but ahead of all of the other Democratic contenders. Richardson has been widely mentioned as a potential vice-presidential running mate, though Richardson has said he would continue serving as New Mexico governor if his presidential campaign faltered.

Tom Vilsack
Former Governor
Iowa

Vilsack announced his presidential candidacy in November 2006, and his chief political strength was his eight years of service as a governor in a politically competitive state in the Midwest. But Vilsack left the race in February 2007, citing difficulty in raising campaign funds. In March 2007, Vilsack endorsed the presidential candidacy of New York Democratic senator Hillary Rodham Clinton, who is expected to consider Vilsack as a possible vice-presidential running mate if she wins the Democratic presidential nomination.

Republican Candidates

Sam Brownback
Senator
Kansas

Prior to his election to the Senate in 1996, Brownback served one term in the U.S. House of Representatives (1995–1996) and also previously served as Kansas' secretary of agriculture (1986–1993). Little known outside his sparsely populated home state, Brownback sought to cultivate socially conservative voters opposed to abortion and same-sex marriage. A former evangelical Christian who is now a Catholic, Brownback competed with Arkansas governor Mike Huckabee in particular for the votes of social-issue conservatives, whom Brownback hoped would propel his candidacy out of the second tier of Republican presidential hopefuls and into more serious contention. But Brownback struggled to raise money or garner much media attention, and he pulled out of the presidential race in October 2007.

James S. Gilmore III
Former Governor
Virginia

Gilmore waged a presidential campaign in which he portrayed himself as the best conservative alternative to front-running Republicans Rudolph W. Giuliani, Mitt Romney, and John McCain, whom Gilmore collectively branded as "Rudy McRomney." Gilmore, who left the Virginia governorship in 2002 after a single four-year term, raised little money for his presidential campaign and was barely visible in early polls of Republican voters. Gilmore withdrew from the race in July 2007 and plans instead to run for a U.S. Senate seat in Virginia in 2008.

Rudolph W. Giuliani
Former Mayor
New York City

Giuliani led the Republican presidential field in national polls in mid-2007. He achieved celebrity status as "America's Mayor" following the September 11, 2001, terrorist attacks that occurred at the end of Giuliani's mayoral tenure. A former federal prosecutor, Giuliani has cultivated an image as someone who could protect the nation from another terrorist attack.

Giuliani's support for abortion rights and gay rights places him to the political left of socially conservative voters who tend to hold sway in Republican primary and caucus elections. Some prominent conservative activists, including James Dobson of Focus on the Family and Tony Perkins of the Family Research Council, have expressed strong reservations to a Giuliani presidential bid. But there is evidence that Giuliani might surmount this opposition: a September 2007 survey by The Pew Research Center found that there was "minimal public awareness of Giuliani's position on abortion" and that "it does not appear that Giuliani's stance has appreciably hurt his image within his party's conservative base."[10] Some conservative Republicans in Congress have backed Giuliani's White House bid. Giuliani was endorsed by Steve Forbes, the conservative publisher who sought the Republican presidential nomination in 1996 and 2000.

Giuliani's backers see him as the most electable Republican in a general election. Giuliani, who won two elections in strongly Democratic-leaning New York City, has noted this himself. "I'm the only Republican candidate that has the chance of winning the states that were previously Democratic states," Giuliani said in St. Paul, Minnesota, in September 2007.[11]

Mike Huckabee
Former Governor
Arkansas

Huckabee's campaign gained some steam in August 2007, when he placed second in a nonbinding "straw poll" of Iowa Republicans. Huckabee finished behind only former Massachusetts governor Mitt Romney, who had invested considerable resources and campaign time to win the straw poll. While the significance of the nonbinding vote was lessened considerably by the decisions of former New York City mayor Rudolph Giuliani and Arizona senator John McCain to skip the straw poll, and by the absence of former Tennessee senator Fred Thompson (who was not a declared candidate at the time), Huckabee sought to parlay his runner-up showing into a more serious campaign for the Republican nomination.

Duncan Hunter
Congressman
California

Hunter, who has represented a congressional district in and around San Diego since 1981, brandishes the expertise in national security policy that he gained as the former chairman of the House Armed Services Committee. A Vietnam War veteran, Hunter is a distinct long shot for the Republican presidential nomination but hopes that a strong showing in the Republican primary in South Carolina (a state with a substantial military presence) will vault him into serious contention.

John McCain
Senator
Arizona

McCain was the chief contender to George W. Bush for the 2000 Republican presidential nomination, and his second White House bid initially attracted support from many who backed Bush's ultimately successful effort in 2000. But McCain endured rocky times in spring and summer 2007 that threatened to mortally wound his campaign. His campaign staff anticipated raising far more money than it actually did, and his staff-heavy effort so hemorrhaged campaign funds that McCain's campaign had just $2 million left to spend at the end of June. McCain's campaign manager resigned and his campaign operations were dramatically streamlined.

While McCain has a generally conservative voting record, his support for an overhaul of immigration laws that many conservatives said was tantamount to giving illegal immigrants "amnesty" has not put him in the good graces of many in his party. And he has faced recurring questions about his advanced age—McCain turned 71 in August 2007—though McCain said that his health is good and that he continues to keep a vigorous schedule in the Senate and on the campaign trail.

McCain sought to regain his political footing in the fall of 2007 with an aggressive and high-profile defense of the Bush administration's so-called troop surge in Iraq. While much of the American public was highly skeptical of the plan, McCain, a Vietnam War veteran who was held captive for five and a half years, said that the troop increase and a change in military strategy in Iraq should be given a chance to succeed under the direction of Army Gen. David H. Petraeus, the top U.S. military commander in Iraq.

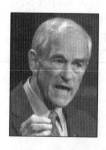

Ron Paul
Congressman
Texas

Paul is an iconoclastic Republican who holds libertarian views; in fact, Paul was the Libertarian Party's presidential candidate in the 1988 election and received 432,000 votes, or about 0.5 percent of the total. Whenever there is a roll call vote in the House with one vote in the "no" column, it almost always belongs to Paul, who regularly votes against appropriations bills and other ostensibly innocuous legislation on the grounds that they are not explicitly authorized by the Constitution. Paul's self-described "non-interventionist" foreign policy includes his opposition to the Iraq war—he was one of just six House Republicans who voted in 2002 against the original war authorization. Paul says his opposition to the Iraq war is in keeping with the classic conservative position to not bring the United States into foreign entanglements. Paul lagged far behind in early polls but enjoyed some success in campaign fundraising, boosted by a surge in small donations. Paul's supporters have promoted their candidate aggressively on Web sites like MySpace.

Mitt Romney
Former Governor
Massachusetts

Polished and handsome, Romney looks like a presidential candidate straight from central casting. He served as governor of Massachusetts for a single four-year term (2003–2007) and declined to seek reelection in 2006—a politically wise decision, for he very well could have lost in the anti-Republican political environment that prevailed that year. Despite his relatively meager political experience, Romney also touts qualifications that included a long background as a venture capitalist and his leading role in helping rescue the 2002 Winter Olympics in Salt Lake City as a replacement chief executive officer.

Romney emphasizes business-oriented conservatism and also courts social-issue conservatives with his opposition to abortion and gay marriage. In 1994, however, Romney had supported abortion rights and gay rights in his unsuccessful Senate campaign against Democratic senator Edward M. Kennedy—something regularly noted by Romney's critics, who accuse him of adopting more conservative positions on social issues for political purposes. Romney has acknowledged holding more liberal positions on social issues in years past but claims the shift in his thinking is sincere. Romney has emerged as a top-tier presidential candidate as a result of his robust fundraising, including his own deep pockets, and for his strong showing in early polls in Iowa and New Hampshire, which traditionally vote first in the nomination contests.

Romney's presidential campaign has also drawn considerable attention for his religious affiliation with the Church of Jesus Christ of Latter-day Saints (better known as the Mormon Church). According to a Pew Forum survey in September 2007, 46 percent of respondents described Romney as "very religious," compared to 43 percent who said that about President Bush and 14 percent who said that about former New York City mayor Rudolph W. Giuliani. One-fourth of Americans said that they would be less likely to vote for a presidential candidate who is Mormon.[12]

Tom Tancredo
Congressman
Colorado

One would be hard-pressed to find a presidential candidate more vigorously opposed to illegal immigration than Tancredo, who was first elected in 1998 to represent Republican-leaning suburbs south of Denver. His presidential effort has received little traction, and he is not expected to pose a serious threat to the better-known and better-funded Republican front-running candidates.

Fred Thompson
Former Senator
Tennessee

It is testimony to how early contemporary presidential campaigns now begin that Thompson's official candidate announcement on September 6, 2007—fully four months before the first primary and caucus voting—sparked debate as to whether Thompson waited too long to officially enter the race. But with many Republican voters expressing dissatisfaction with their choices of presidential candidates in the spring and summer of 2007, Thompson sensed a void that he sought to fill. He is expected to run especially strongly in the presidential primaries and caucuses in the South.

Thompson's claim to fame as an actor-politician—his service in the Senate (1994–2003) was sandwiched by an earlier movie career and a more recent run as the New York district attorney Arthur Branch on the NBC drama *Law and Order*—spawned comparisons between Thompson and former Republican president Ronald Reagan, another former actor. Yet Thompson has some liabilities as a candidate, including a reputation that he is a less than energetic campaigner.

Tommy Thompson
Former Secretary
U.S. Health and Human Services
Former Governor
Wisconsin

Thompson, who is not related to Fred Thompson, has long wanted to be president. During his short-lived White House campaign, Thompson wielded an impressive and long public service resume that included serving two decades in the Wisconsin legislature; fourteen years as Wisconsin's governor; and four years as President Bush's secretary of Health and Human Services.

Thompson struggled to raise campaign cash or garner much attention in such a crowded Republican field. He had hoped to use Iowa, which abuts Wisconsin, as a springboard to more serious contention, but Thompson withdrew from the Republican presidential race on August 12, 2007—one day after Thompson won just 1 percent of the vote and finished sixth in a nonbinding "straw poll" of Iowa Republicans.[13]

Role of Front Loading

One of the most notable characteristics about the 2008 presidential campaign was the highly accelerated calendar under which many states planned to vote for their nominees—more than six months before their respective national party conventions.

For much of our nation's history, presidential nominations were actually decided at the national conventions a few months before the general election. Those were the days before the widespread use of primary elections—the current system—to determine delegate allocations. It has been more than thirty years since a national convention was suspenseful or influential in selecting a major party nominee—the 1976 Republican nomination in Kansas City, where President Gerald R. Ford narrowly outpolled former California governor Ronald Reagan. Since then, however, the conventions have served mainly to coronate candidates whose nominations were clinched months earlier and to allow the national parties to burnish their images and promote their policy views to a national television audience.

It is possible that the 2008 Democratic and Republican presidential nominees will be known as early as February of that year—more than six months before the Democratic convention in Denver (August 25–28) and the Republican convention in St. Paul, Minnesota (September 1–4). Yet it is also plausible that the early February contests might produce a split outcome, and that the nominations could be decided a few weeks later.

In early 2007, numerous state legislatures moved to enact legislation to move their 2008 presidential primaries and caucuses to early February. Under the rules of the Republican National Committee (RNC) and the Democratic National Committee (DNC), nearly every state had to hold its 2008 presidential primary or caucus on or after February 5. (The Democratic Party rules have long granted exemptions to Iowa and New Hampshire, and for the 2008 election the DNC also allowed Nevada and South Carolina to hold contests before February 5. RNC rules do not grant exemptions.) In March 2007, California Republican Governor Arnold Schwarzenegger signed legislation that moved his state's 2008 presidential primary to February 5—four months earlier than the June 5 date mandated by the previous state law. Schwarzenegger said that advancing the date of the presidential election in his state, the nation's most populous, "means California will have the influence it deserves in choosing America's next presidential candidates."[14]

One month later, in April 2007, New York Democratic governor Eliot Spitzer signed a bill to advance his state's 2008 presidential primary to February 5. New York previously held its presidential primary in March. Spitzer said that a February primary in New York, the nation's third most-populous state, "will help secure New York's large and diverse population an influential voice in selecting the 2008 presidential nominees."[15] The move was also intended to boost the presidential campaigns of the two major candidates from New York—Hillary Rodham Clinton and Rudolph W. Giuliani. Not to be outdone, the Illinois Democrats who control that state's legislature established a February 5, 2008, presidential primary to give Illinois more clout in the presidential nomination prospects—but also to boost the White House campaign of Barack Obama.

Some officials were so determined to hold early primary or caucus contests in their states that they were prepared to flout the rules of their national party committees, which are empowered to strip their state party affiliates of national convention delegates if they schedule their 2008 nomination contests to be held earlier than February 5. In May 2007, Florida Republican governor Charlie Crist signed a bill, passed by the Republican-controlled legislature with the support of many Democrats, that set a 2008 presidential primary election for January 29—exactly one week before the February 5 cutoff date.[16] Florida Democratic officials importuned the DNC to allow them to use the January 29, 2008, primary to apportion its convention delegates, but the party's rule-making panel in August 2007 decided to eliminate Florida's Democratic convention delegate allotment unless it scheduled a binding primary or caucus to be held on or after Feb 5. RNC rules allowed national party officials to cut the Florida Republican convention delegation by half.

Even before the first primary votes were cast in early 2008, the heavily front-loaded schedule of primary and caucus elections sparked renewed calls to overhaul how the national political parties nominate their presidential nominees. It was a common refrain in 2007 that the presidential selection process is "broken." Some common complaints are that the nomination process begins too early and is too heavily reliant on raising and spending money, and that it does not promote personal, one-on-one communication between presidential candidates and voters.

Although the 2008 presidential election promised to feature more early nomination contests than ever, front-loading itself is not a novelty. It has its genesis in the early 1970s, when changes to political party rules accelerated the use of presidential primary elections instead of caucuses, many of which had been dominated by state political "kingmakers" who could engineer the selection of the eventual nominee at the national convention. Detractors said the nomination process should be made more democratic and allow voters to have more political power than political insiders. In 1968, fewer than one-third of the states held presidential primary elections; by 2000, more than forty states held presidential primary elections.

"The growth in presidential primaries quickly changed the whole dynamic of the nominating process," suggested political analyst Rhodes Cook. "In the convention-oriented system of the previous half century, the few primaries in existence served as a vehicle for candidates to showcase their vote-getting appeal. But primaries then could only advance a candidate's cause. It was at the conventions where the choices were made, and it was the party leaders that had the final say there."[17] As more states began holding presidential primary elections, they scheduled them earlier in the election year so as to maximize media attention, voter turnout, and visits from the candidates themselves. Efforts by the national political parties to rein in frontloading—either by stripping convention delegates from state affiliates that engage in the practice or by offering extra convention delegates to state affiliates that do not—have proven futile.

Numerous individuals and organizations have proposed a variety of plans to Congress and the national political parties to overhaul the presidential nomination process. The National Association of Secretaries of State (NASS), an organization that comprises the chief election officials in the fifty states, has long promoted a plan of regional rotating presidential primary elections that would divide the country into four regions of equal population. All of the states in one region would hold their primaries or caucuses on a fixed day a few weeks before the states in the next region would vote. The region that voted first in one election year would vote last in the next cycle, while the region that had voted second would rotate forward to vote first in the subsequent cycle.

The front-loading frenzy has even drawn the attention and concern of Congress. Michigan Democratic representative Sander M. Levin has long promoted legislation to overhaul the presidential primary process by dividing the nation into six regions, then further dividing them into six sub-regions, each of which would be composed of one or more states from each of the six regions. The six sub-regions would vote on six specific dates in a presidential election year, with one sub-region voting two or three weeks before the next sub-region. Levin in March 2007 called his legislation a "long overdue step towards fixing the broken system of the Presidential primary and caucus schedule."[18]

In 2000, the Republican National Committee (RNC) came close to overhauling the presidential primary process. The RNC that year gave initial approval to the so-called Delaware Plan, which organized the states to allow lesser-populous states to vote before more populous states. But the plan ultimately was rejected at the 2000 Republican national convention in Philadelphia, as Bush campaign aides did not want the prospect of a floor fight to disrupt the convention's clockwork planning. "It had nothing to do with the merits of the Delaware Plan," said Tom Sansonetti, a Wyoming lawyer who was the chairman of the RNC Rules Committee in 2000. "It was just that the convention was scripted, and there was no room for a three-hour floor fight on whether or not the Delaware Plan should be adopted or whether the party was going to stay with its present system."[19]

Fundraising

In this day and age, presidential campaigns require raising a substantial amount of money. Copious amounts of campaign funds are needed to pay for staff; to air television and radio advertisements; to print campaign signs and mail communications; to shuttle the candidate and staff all over the country; and for other things. Raising money is a grueling process. There are strict limits on how much money an individual donor can give to a candidate for a federal office; for the 2008 election year, the limit was $2,300 for a primary election and $2,300 for a general election, for a total of $4,600.[20]

There is no hard-and-fast rule that posits how much money a presidential campaign needs to be successful. While any candidate prefers to have more money than less, some candidates can manage and thrive on lean budgets and other candidates have failed despite raising a lot of money. Still, some political analysts thought that a candidate for the 2008 presidential nomination needed to have raised $20 million in 2007 to be deemed credible. Several candidates shattered that threshold at the halfway point of 2007, and the candidates easily topped all previous records for presidential election fundraising. According to the nonpartisan and independent Campaign Finance Institute, candidates for president in 2008 raised more money ($277 million) for the primary elections in the first half of 2007 than the candidates for president in 2004 raised for all of calendar year 2003.[21] The field was topped by Hillary Rodham Clinton, whose $91 million in total receipts for the first nine months of 2007 included $10 million from her Senate campaign account. Barack Obama raised $80 million in the first nine months of 2007.

The top fund-raisers on the Republican side were Mitt Romney, whose $62.8 million raised through the end of September 2007 included $17.4 million in personal loans from the candidate, and Rudolph W. Giuliani, who raised $47.3 million in the first nine months of 2007.

Not only were the candidates raising substantial amounts of money, they were spending it too—in part because the heavily "front-loaded" calendar of presidential primaries and caucuses in early 2008 required significant investments early on. Romney spent $53.6 million in the first nine months of 2007, or more than 85 percent of his receipts. His campaign defended the big early spending on the grounds that Romney was not as well-known nationwide as Giuliani or John McCain, and that investments were needed in the early-voting states of Iowa and New Hampshire. McCain reported spending $28.6 million of the $32.1 million he raised—a "burn rate" of 89 percent. That has left McCain with little money in the bank, and he has drastically curtailed his campaign staff and other expenses.

The Playing Field

A presidential campaign is a national race, of course, but it is more technically accurate to describe it as a collection of individual contests in each of the fifty states, nearly all of which give the popular vote winner all of its electoral votes. Presidential campaigns have pollsters who regularly gauge political preferences of voters to determine which states are most deserving of their attention. Polling data will drive decisions where candidates will campaign, air television and radio advertisements, and hire paid campaign organizers in states that appear to be closely contended and will shift resources away from states that do not appear to be politically competitive.

Some voters have bemoaned the tendency of presidential candidates to target a disproportionate amount of their campaign funds and candidate visits in a relatively small number of states. The decision to campaign in only those states that are "in play" in the presidential election can leave millions of voters feeling ignored in the race for the most powerful and influential office in the world.

As a case in point, little formal presidential campaigning transpires in New York state. This is because New York has backed the Democratic presidential nominee in each of the past five presidential elections—and by overwhelming margins. Republicans see little utility in committing resources to a state that will almost certainly not vote for their presidential candidates, and Democrats need not waste their time and money in a state that is going to vote for them anyway. The roles are reversed in many states in the Mountain West and Great Plains that are so strongly Republican that Democratic presidential candidates scarcely campaign there.

Even though the 2004 presidential election was very close—President Bush defeated John Kerry by less than 3 percentage points in the national popular vote tally—

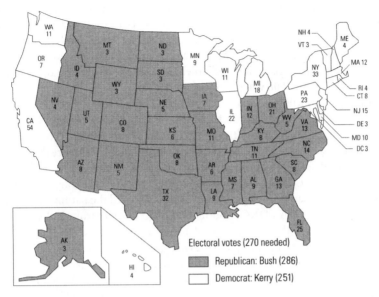

FIGURE 2
Presidential General Election Map, 2004

Note: Minnesota has ten electoral votes; one elector voted for Sen. John Edwards, D-N.C., for president.

Source: "Figure 1-4 Presidential General Election Map, 2004" CQ Electronic Library, CQ's Vital Statistics on American Politics Online Edition, vsap05–fig1-4. Originally published in Harold W. Stanley and Richard G. Niemi, *Vital Statistics on American Politics* 2005–2006 (Washington: CQ Press, 2006). http://library.cqpress.com/vsap05_fig1-4 (accessed October 3, 2007).

the contests in a majority of the states were not close. In 26 states and in the District of Columbia, the winning candidate won by more than 12 percentage points. Many states that were closely contested in the 2004 presidential election almost certainly will be vigorously contested in 2008. These include the Upper Midwestern states of Wisconsin and Iowa. In 2004, Wisconsin backed Kerry by four-tenths of one percentage point and Iowa sided with Bush by seven-tenths of one percentage point. The Mountain West states of New Mexico, Colorado, and Nevada all backed President Bush by less than 5 percentage points in the 2004 election and surely will be up for grabs in the 2008 contest. Among the more populous states with larger electoral vote allocations, it seems certain that the presidential candidates will actively contest Ohio, which was the pivotal state in the 2004 election, and Florida, which held that claim to fame more controversially in the 2000 election between Bush and Vice President Al Gore.

Role of the Parties and Interest Groups

The Republican and Democratic nominees will be the chief actors in the 2008 presidential campaign and the primary communicators with the voters. But there will be other political players who will influence the race. They include the Republican National Committee (RNC) and the Democratic National Committee (DNC) and their affiliate party organizations at the state and local level. The RNC and DNC are tasked primarily with overseeing the party's strategy in presidential elections, including fundraising and voter registration and voter turnout efforts leading up to and on Election Day (which in 2008 will be November 4).

Other key players will be so-called 527 political organizations that are named for the section of the federal tax code under which they incorporate. Unlike federal candidates and political action committees (PACs), which receive limited contributions, 527 organizations can accept unlimited funds that they use to influence the nomination, election, or defeat of political candidates. In the past few years, many 527 political organizations have filled a void that was created by a 2002 campaign finance law, known as the Bipartisan Campaign Reform Act, that barred the national party committees (like the RNC and DNC) and federal officeholders from collecting "soft money," which refers to the largely unregulated funds upon which the political parties came to rely for party-building activities like get-out-the-vote efforts and generic issue-based political advertising. Wealthy individuals who gave large "soft money" donations to the national political parties shifted their money to 527 organizations.

In the 2004 presidential election, some of the more prominent 527 organizations included the Swift Boat Veterans for Truth, which aired television commercials that were sharply critical of Democratic nominee John Kerry's military service during the Vietnam War, and America Votes, a collection of liberal-leaning organizations that concentrated on voter registration and turnout efforts. Advocacy groups that are active in the 2008 presidential election include MoveOn.org Political Action, a liberal PAC of about 3.3 million members. Formed in response to the impeachment of President Bill Clinton, MoveOn.org advocates a number of liberal causes and vigorously opposed the war in Iraq. MoveOn.org was criticized by most Republicans and some Democrats in the summer and fall of 2007, after the group ran a full-page advertisement in the *New York Times* that criticized Gen. David H. Petraeus, the top U.S. military commander in Iraq, with the provocative headline "General Petraeus or General Betray Us?"

The AFL-CIO and the U.S. Chamber of Commerce are among the other organizations that will have well-developed political strategies for the 2008 campaign. The League of Conservation Voters and the Sierra Club will support candidates who share their views on environmental policy. EMILY's List, a powerful PAC that backs Democratic women candidates who support pro-choice rights, has a large network of donors that it hopes will help elect Hillary Clinton as this country's first woman president.

Role of the Internet

The Internet has played a larger role from one election to the next, and the 2008 campaign will continue the trend. Presidential and congressional campaigns, national party committees, and interest groups increasingly look to the Internet as an efficient and relatively inexpensive way of raising money and disseminating campaign com-

Barack Obama's presidential campaign had nothing to do with it, but the Illinois Democrat got plenty of publicity from the release of a Web video, posted to the popular file-sharing site YouTube, that featured an attractive young woman singing seductively about how she has "got a crush on Obama." As of October 2007, the video had been viewed more than 3.8 million times.

munications. More than ever, political campaigns are hiring staff members whose primary responsibilities are to boost the campaigns' online presence. Candidates for president in 2008 constructed pages on MySpace and Facebook, two popular social networking sites that are especially popular with younger voters who tend to vote less regularly than older voters.

In January 2007, Hillary Clinton actually announced her presidential candidacy online, saying in a video message on her campaign Web site that she was "beginning a conversation—with you, with America." [22] In September 2007, Fred Thompson released a video announcement that confirmed his formal entry in the Republican presidential contest. [23] The growing role of the Internet in campaign politics also was demonstrated in a July 2007 Democratic presidential debate that was sponsored by CNN and YouTube, the video-sharing Web site that allows users to post and view video messages. The July 23 debate featured questions that were submitted by YouTube users. CNN and YouTube planned a Republican debate for November 2007.

Presidential and congressional candidates are raising more of their campaign funds online. While the funds that are itemized on campaign finance reports do not indicate how those monies were raised, it is clear that candidates for office and the political parties are making greater use of the Internet to raise money for political purposes.

Democrats have outperformed Republicans in raising campaign funds online. On the Democratic side, the Web site ActBlue includes a catalog of party candidates all across the nation and allows users to contribute online to their preferred candidates. Republicans have acknowledged that they lag behind the Democrats in online fundraising. In 2006, some Republican activists created the Web site Rightroots.com to allow Republican donors to contribute to their candidates of choice.

As more and more Americans go online to receive their news and other information, blogs are becoming more influential players in the political process. Many of these online journals have a defined and aggressive partisan slant. Some of them have large audiences, and it is more common to see bloggers included as part of the credentialed press that cover press conferences and major campaign events, including the national presidential conventions. Congressional leaders and their staffs are in frequent contact with prominent bloggers with whom they largely see eye-to-eye and who have substantial readerships. An online story publicized by Matt Drudge, the online journalist who runs the widely read "Drudge Report," can drive substantial Web traffic to the originating publication and attract attention from mainstream media outlets like newspapers and television stations.

Third-Party Candidates?

Every presidential election, the overwhelming number of people who vote back either the Democratic or the Republican nominee. But there are millions of voters are disgusted with the two-party system and do not vote. Many of them express interest in candidates who run as other than the nominees of the Democratic or Republican parties. Yet in modern history no independent or third-party candidate has ever won a presidential election—or even come close to doing so. The Democratic and Republican parties have coexisted for more than 150 years, and the presidential nominees of the two major parties have enormous institutional advantages over candidates who are not affiliated with either party. Ballot-access laws are onerous for candidates who are not Republicans or Democrats. Third-party candidates struggle to garner much attention in the media and are routinely excluded from presidential and congressional debates. And candidates who do not run as Democrats or Republicans often are cast as "spoilers" who have no chance of victory. This hampered the 2004 presidential campaign of Ralph Nader, whom many Democratic activists claim helped tip the presidential election from Al Gore to George W. Bush in 2000. Bush won the pivotal Florida contest by a 537-vote margin that was substantially smaller than the 97,488 votes Nader won from individuals who presumably would have been more sympathetic to Gore than to Bush, had Nader not been a factor in the election.

Notwithstanding those daunting obstacles, individuals and organizations sympathetic to more candidate choices in presidential elections continue to promote the idea. One of the more notable efforts to field a third-option presidential ticket in 2008 was organized by the group Unity08, a centrist independent group that sought to form a bipartisan presidential ticket. Unity08 was founded by a veteran, bipartisan team—Democrats Gerald Rafshoon and Hamilton Jordan, who helped Georgia Democrat Jimmy Carter win the presidency in 1976, and Doug Bailey, who retired as a Republican operative in the 1980s. Unity08's public face is the actor Sam Waterston, who is best-known for playing executive assistant district attorney Jack McCoy on the long-running NBC drama *Law and Order*. (Interestingly, 2008 Republican candidate Fred Thompson played McCoy's district attorney boss on the program). Waterson said in April 2007 that an outsider president "could summon the congressional leadership of both parties and both houses to the White House, shut the doors and get serious about finding answers they can all agree on." [24]

By June 2008, Unity08 plans to come up with five potential tickets, each one with a presidential candidate of one party and a running mate from some other party. The final Unity08 nominees will then be chosen in an online election open to all registered voters. Well before then, there was rampant speculation about just which prospective candidates might form this third-option ticket. One prominent name mentioned was Michael Bloomberg, the mayor of New York City. Bloomberg was a lifelong liberal Democrat who changed his political affiliation to Republican prior to his election in 2001. In 2007, Bloomberg became a political independent and traveled the nation to speak about national issues, sparking speculation that he was interested in running for president in 2008. "We need real solutions that honestly address the big challenges we face as a nation," Bloomberg said in September 2007. "For too long, the American people have been served up empty promises based on what politicians think we want to hear. It's time for something real." [25]

Despite sounding and acting like a presidential candidate, Bloomberg repeatedly has said that he would not seek the White House in 2008. But his political advisers nonetheless have promoted the idea. Perhaps Bloomberg's biggest political asset is his vast personal wealth: he is a billionaire and philanthropist who self-financed his successful mayoral campaigns in 2001 and 2005. Bloomberg has the vast financial resources needed to wage a national campaign independent of the two-party system.

Chuck Hagel, a Republican senator from Nebraska, also was prominently mentioned in 2007 as a potential candidate for president—either as a Republican or as a maverick. Hagel's politics are generally conservative, but in recent months he has emerged as a maverick Republican for his strong opposition to the Bush administration's strategy in Iraq. But Hagel said in September 2007 that he was retiring from politics altogether at the end of 2008 and would not be a candidate for the presidency. Sam Nunn, a former Democratic senator from Georgia, also was mentioned as a potential independent presidential candidate in 2008. Nunn served in the Senate from 1972 through 1996, when he retired at just 58 years old. He concentrated in national security policy as the chairman of the Senate Armed Services Committee. Nunn's voting record placed him on the conservative spectrum of the Democratic Party.

At this writing, it is unclear how influential Unity08 will be in the 2008 presidential campaign. Any significant third-party campaign requires substantial financial resources, ample media attention, and a compelling candidate as its standard-bearer. "This is a very, very major organizational undertaking," said Larry Jacobs, a political scientist at the University of Minnesota. "It's like building an army from scratch. And how you do that without significant resources—organizational resources, monetary resources, intellectual resources—it's daunting."[26]

2008 Congressional Races

Coinciding with the 2008 presidential race will be pitched battles for control of the House and the Senate. Throughout 2007, Democrats appeared more likely than not to retain their majorities in the House and the Senate, though Republicans promised to aggressively challenge the Democrats.

Democratic and Republican candidates alike will run as agents of "change" in the 2008 election because the vast majority of voters were highly dissatisfied with how things are going in this country. According to the July 2007 Battleground Poll conducted by the Democratic firm Lake Research Partners and the Republican firm The Tarrance Group, 70 percent of registered likely voters in the 2008 election felt that things in this country are on the "wrong track," compared to just 21 percent who felt that things are on the "right track." This was the most lopsided margin in many years. Disaffected voters also found fault with the performance of both major parties. The Battleground Poll found that 52 percent of respondents disapproved of the new Democratic-led Congress—but even greater majorities disapproved of the job performances of congressional Republicans (61 percent) and President Bush (61 percent). Many voters who disapproved of the Democrats said they hadn't done enough to challenge Bush's policies in Iraq.

Nonetheless, Democrats enjoyed some early successes in the 2007–2008 campaign cycle. Republicans were demoralized after the 2006 elections and were just beginning to regroup in 2007. Democrats outperformed Republicans in candidate recruitment and fundraising. Democratic candidates also stood to benefit from continued public opposition to President Bush and his policies, specifically the Iraq War. Republican strategists noted that Bush will not be on the ballot in 2008 and were hopeful that their party will be defined less by Bush and more by the party's presidential nominee. They also said that the Democrats would be in a defensive crouch in 2008 because they would have to answer for their record as the majority party.

House Races

House Democrats began the 110th Congress (2007–2008) with 233 House seats, compared to 202 for the Republicans. Because 218 House seats comprise a majority of the 435-member House, the Republicans will need to make a net gain of 16 House seats above the 202 they presently hold if they want to reclaim a majority of House seats in 2008.

Armed with majority status, House Democrats moved out to a big fundraising advantage over their Republican counterparts in 2007. In the first nine months of 2007, the Democratic Congressional Campaign Committee (DCCC), the campaign arm of House Democrats, reported raising $52.6 million, compared to $37.2 million for its partisan counterpart, the National Republican Congressional Committee (NRCC). The

TABLE 2 2004 Presidential Vote of Districts of House Freshmen Democrats

REPRESENTATIVE	STATE (DISTRICT)	PERCENTAGE OF VOTE FOR BUSH IN 2004
Harry E. Mitchell	AZ (5)	54
Gabrielle Giffords	AZ (8)	53
Jerry McNerney	CA (11)	54
Ed Perlmutter	CO (7)	48
Joe Courtney	CT (2)	44
Christopher S. Murphy	CT (5)	49
Kathy Castor	FL (11)	40
Tim Mahoney	FL (16)	55
Ron Klein	FL (22)	49
Hank Johnson	GA (4)	28
Mazie K. Hirono	HI (2)	44
Phil Hare	IL (17)	48
Joe Donnelly	IN (2)	56
Brad Ellsworth	IN (8)	62
Baron P. Hill	IN (9)	59
Bruce Braley	IA (1)	46
David Loebsack	IA (2)	44
Nancy Boyda	KS (2)	59
John Yarmuth	KY (3)	49
John Sarbanes	MD (3)	45
Tim Walz	MN (1)	51
Keith Ellison	MN (5)	28
Carol Shea-Porter	NH (1)	51
Paul W. Hodes	NH (2)	47
Albio Sires	NJ (13)	31
Yvette D. Clarke	NY (11)	13

continues

TABLE 2 2004 Presidential Vote of Districts of House Freshmen Democrats (cont.)

REPRESENTATIVE	STATE (DISTRICT)	PERCENTAGE OF VOTE FOR BUSH IN 2004
John Hall	NY (19)	53
Kirsten Gillibrand	NY (20)	53
Michael Arcuri	NY (24)	52
Heath Shuler	NC (11)	57
Charlie Wilson	OH (6)	50
Betty Sutton	OH (13)	44
Zack Space	OH (18)	57
Jason Altmire	PA (4)	54
Joe Sestak	PA (7)	47
Patrick Murphy	PA (8)	48
Christopher Carney	PA (10)	60
Steve Cohen	TN (9)	29
Nick Lampson	TX (22)	64
Ciro D. Rodriguez	TX (23)	57
Peter Welch	VT (AL)	39
Steve Kagen	WI (8)	55

Note: Districts won by President Bush in 2004 are shaded.

Source: Adapted from *CQ Weekly*'s "Class of 2006" http://www.cq.com/members/factfilereport.do?report=mff-frosh and "2004 Presidential Vote by House District, 110th Congress (2007–2008)" http://www.cqpolitics.com/pdfs/2004PresidentialVotebyCD.pdf.

DCCC's advantage in available cash-on-hand was even more lopsided: at the end of September, the DCCC had $28.3 million left to spend, compared to just $1.6 million for the NRCC.[27] This imbalance will allow the DCCC to wage serious bids in Republican-held districts and to shore up Democratic members who were narrowly elected or reelected in 2006.

Throughout 2007 and into the 2008 election year, Republican strategists focused primarily on securing political opposition for many of the forty-two Democrats who were first elected in 2006.[28] Exactly half of them—twenty-one—won in districts that just two years earlier had backed President Bush's reelection. These districts included Indiana's 8th District, where Democrat Brad Ellsworth was elected in a district that gave Bush 62 percent of its votes in the 2004 election, and Pennsylvania's 10th District, where Democrat Christopher Carney was victorious in a district that had given President Bush 60 percent of the vote.

Yet many of these Democratic freshmen endeavored early in their first terms to bolster their political standing back home. No sooner do freshmen members of Congress arrive for orientation in Washington than do political party officials prevail upon them to begin raising campaign funds. Party leaders generally counsel their freshmen members from politically competitive districts to raise plenty of money early so that they deter potentially strong opponents from running—and to be very well-funded in the event serious challengers do surface.

New York freshman Democratic representative Kirsten Gillibrand raised $1.4 million for her 2008 reelection campaign in the first six months of 2007—more than any other first-term member of the House and more than all but two other members in the entire 435-member House.[29] Gillibrand raised money at a breakneck pace because she represents a traditionally Republican-leaning district in upstate New York that Republicans will be trying to win back in the 2008 election. Several Republicans committed early in 2007 to challenging Gillibrand.

According to the Federal Election Commission (FEC), candidates for the House and the Senate in 2008 raised $239 million in the first six months of 2007. House candidates reported raising $157.8 million and Senate candidates raised $80.6 million.[30]

Senate Races

The Republicans began the 2008 Senate campaign holding forty-nine seats in the one-hundred-seat Senate—just two short of a fifty-one-seat majority. But this close margin is misleading and is belied by some significant political obstacles that faced Senate Republican campaign strategists as they went about preparing for the 2008 campaign. Unlike the House, whose 435 members face the voters every two years, just one-third of the Senate is up for election every two-year election cycle. And the partisan distribution of the Senate seats that are contested in an election year need not match the partisan distribution of the entire Senate. While the Republicans hold a forty-nine-seat Senate minority, they began the 2007–2008 election cycle having to defend twenty-one seats in the 2008 election, compared to just twelve for the Democrats. The reason for the big partisan imbalance is that so many Republicans won contests in 2002, when the GOP ended an eighteen-month period of Democratic control of the Senate, and so the Republicans must defend all of those seats six years later, in 2008.

The June 2007 death of Wyoming Republican senator Craig Thomas meant that Republicans would have to defend a twenty-second seat in November 2008. Thomas's appointed successor, Republican John A. Barrasso, planned to run in a special election that was required by state law to fill the remaining four years of the term Thomas originally won in November 2006. "We have 22 seats to defend. The Democrats only have 12 seats to defend. We knew going in that this was going to be a tough election cycle for us," John Ensign, chairman of the NRSC, said in September 2007 on the ABC program *This Week*. Ensign added, "But the good thing is that we have good people in place" to contest races.[31]

On the same program, DSCC chief Charles Schumer said that "the wind is at our backs" and that Democrats were poised to win in states that are politically "red," the color frequently used by many political analysts to describe states that usually vote

Republican. "Because the people want change so much, change in Iraq, change to help the middle class, change in the ethical climate in Washington, we have opportunities in states that we never thought we would in deeply red states throughout the country," Schumer said.

Senate Democrats through 2007 were much better-funded than their Republican counterparts. In the first nine months of 2007, the DSCC reported raising $42 million, as compared to the receipts raised by the DSCC's partisan counterpart, the NRSC, which brought in $23.4 million during the period. The Senate Democrats' campaign organization had an even more lopsided advantage in campaign cash on hand. At the beginning of October 2007, the DSCC had $22.9 million left to spend, compared to $8.3 million for the NRSC. The DSCC has such a huge advantage because it spent a much smaller share of its receipts than did the NRSC.

The cash-on-hand numbers are important because the DSCC and NRSC are allowed to spend unlimited sums on "independent expenditures," which are outlays that the national party committees can spend on advertisements to attack the opposition or promote their preferred candidates, so long as the ads are not made in consultation or cooperation with the candidates' campaigns. In previous election cycles, national party committees have spent sums on independent expenditures in races that rival or even exceed what the candidates themselves raise and spend—and their advertisements, while technically "independent" of what the candidates do, can influence the tenor, issue discussion, and the outcome of races.

The Democrats have a more pronounced advantage over Republicans in campaign fundraising in the 2007–2008 campaign cycle, when they held a majority in Congress, than in the 2005–2006 campaign cycle, when the Republicans were in control of Congress. This shift is not surprising, for a political party that is in control of Congress and sets the policy agenda generally is more successful at raising money than the political party that is not in the majority and is effectively powerless to affect the policy agenda.

Republican-Held Seats

The DSCC planned to parlay its fundraising advantage to compete vigorously in a handful of the 22 Senate contests in which Republicans are the defending party. They include Virginia, where Republican senator John Warner announced in August 2007 that he would not seek a fifth Senate term in 2008. Warner was such a popular figure in Virginia politics that the Democrats did not even field a challenger to oppose him in 2002, and the senator surely would have been easily reelected in 2008. But Warner's retirement paved the way for former governor Mark Warner (no relation), the state's most visible and popular Democrat, to run as the party's candidate. Mark Warner was the early favorite in the 2008 Senate race in Virginia, even though the state has voted Republican in ten consecutive presidential elections from 1964 to 2004. But Democrats were emboldened by a string of election victories that included Democrat Tim Kaine's election as governor in 2005 (succeeding Mark Warner) and the defeat by Democrat Jim Webb of Republican senator George Allen in 2006.

Less than two weeks after Warner announced his retirement, Nebraska Republican Chuck Hagel said that he would not seek reelection in 2008. Hagel would have been an overwhelming favorite had he chosen to seek a third six-year term in 2008. Nebraska votes strongly Republican in presidential elections, but Democrats have had some success in Senate races in that state. Another highly competitive Senate race appeared likely in Colorado, where two-term Republican senator Wayne Allard announced in January 2007 that he would not seek reelection in 2008. Allard's decision was not unexpected, as he had previously promised to voluntarily limit his Senate service to two terms. It seemed clear that the two party nominees would be Democratic representative Mark Udall, a liberal from Boulder who represents that city and some Denver suburbs and Colorado's ski communities, and Republican former representative Bob Schaffer, a conservative who represented northern and eastern Colorado from 1997 through 2002. Schaffer ran for the U.S. Senate in 2004 but lost the Republican primary election.

Several Republican senators who plan to seek reelection in 2008 face stiff challenges from Democrats. In Minnesota, Republican senator Norm Coleman is facing a difficult reelection campaign in a state that has voted Democratic in every presidential election since 1976—the longest such streak in the nation. The 2008 Senate contest in Minnesota will be Coleman's first reelection campaign to the Senate, following a highly unusual 2002 campaign in which he narrowly defeated Democrat Walter F. Mondale, who was the stand-in Democratic candidate after Democratic senator Paul Wellstone was killed in a plane crash shortly before the November election. Coleman's likely opposition is Al Franken, the comedian, author, and radio talk-show host who achieved fame on the NBC program *Saturday Night Live,* or Michael Ciresi, a wealthy attorney who lost a Democratic primary for the U.S. Senate in 2000. In 2007, Franken has had strong success raising campaign money from liberal activists all across the country.

The Democrats also plan to vigorously contest New Hampshire, where Republican senator John E. Sununu is seeking a second term. Long a Republican bastion in Democratic-leaning New England, New Hampshire has in recent years drifted Democratic, backing John Kerry for president in 2004 and overwhelmingly reelecting Democratic governor John Lynch in 2006. Sununu expects to face former governor Jeanne Shaheen in a rematch of a 2002 campaign that Sununu won by 5 percentage points in a political environment that was more pro-Republican than it is today. Shaheen has been leading Sununu in polls. Other Republican senators who expect serious challenges in 2008 include Susan Collins of Maine, who faces a challenge by Democratic representative Tom Allen, and Gordon Smith of Oregon, where the likely Democratic nominee is Oregon House Speaker Jeff Merkley.

Democrats in 2007 have even talked about a challenge to Kentucky senator Mitch McConnell, the leader of the minority Republicans. While he was overwhelmingly reelected to a fourth term in 2002, a more favorable political environment for Democrats and the likelihood that a serious Democratic challenger would emerge created some problems for him in the summer of 2007. Democratic strategists have sought to paint McConnell as an "obstructionist" to party goals like withdrawing U.S. troops from Iraq.

Democratic-Held Seats

Not only are the Democrats defending far fewer seats than the Republicans in the 2008 election, they also have fewer seats that appear seriously vulnerable to partisan takeover than the Republicans. In just two states are Democratic senators expected to face serious reelection challenges in November 2008—Louisiana, where two-term senator Mary Landrieu is seeking a third term, and South Dakota, where two-term senator Tim Johnson is running after a long recovery from a brain hemorrhage that he suffered in December 2006.

Landrieu expected to face a potentially challenging race in part because her first two contests were very close. In 1996, Landrieu was elected to the Senate by just 5,788 votes out of 1.7 million cast—the slimmest margin ever in a Louisiana Senate race. In 2002, Landrieu won by less than 4 percentage points in a runoff election that was held after she failed to win a majority of voters in a unique nonpartisan primary election. (Beginning in 2008, Louisiana has switched to a system of separate party primaries in federal elections).

But Landrieu also began her 2008 reelection campaign with several advantages. She focused intensely on helping New Orleans secure billions of dollars in federal reconstruction money to assist an area that had been devastated by Hurricane Katrina in 2005. She also had one of the least-liberal voting records among Senate Democrats. Also, the Republican effort to recruit a challenger against Landrieu started slowly, as the GOP focused more attention in 2007 on winning that year's election for governor. On the Republican side, a potential Senate candidate was state treasurer John Kennedy, a former Democrat whose switch to the Republican Party in August 2007 stoked speculation that he would run for the Senate.

South Dakota's Johnson expected a potentially competitive race even before he suffered a brain hemorrhage in December 2006. He returned to the Senate nine months later and said that he planned to seek reelection in 2008. Of the twelve states with Senate contests that Democrats are defending, none backed President Bush's reelection in 2004 more strongly than South Dakota, which gave Bush 60 percent of the vote. Johnson had been reelected to a second term in 2002 by just 524 votes over Republican John Thune, who two years later would defeat Senate Democratic leader Tom Daschle for the state's other Senate seat.

Johnson's illness and long recuperation had the effect of postponing the breakneck fundraising and smash-mouth campaigning that is typical in so many political contests. But surrogates for Johnson raised campaign money for him as he recovered, and the senator actually had more campaign cash-on-hand at the end of June 2007 than he had at a similar point six years earlier, during the run-up to his highly competitive 2002 campaign against Thune. None of the other ten Democratic senators up for reelection in 2008 expect to face such highly competitive contests.

2008 Gubernatorial Races

The 2008 election year also will feature elections for governor in eleven states. The vast majority of state governors face the voters in presidential midterm election years (2002, 2006, 2010, etc.). New Hampshire and Vermont elect governors to two-year terms, so their elections for governor are held each two-year election cycle. The eleven states that have elections for governor in 2008 are Delaware, Indiana, Missouri, Montana, New Hampshire, North Carolina, North Dakota, Utah, Vermont, Washington, and West Virginia. The Democrats are the defending party in six states, while the Republicans are the defending party in the other five.

One of the most highly visible elections for governor in 2008 will be in Missouri, where Republican governor Matt Blunt is expected to face Democratic state attorney

TABLE 3 2007, 2008, and 2009 Gubernatorial Elections

STATE	YEAR OF RACE	DEFENDING PARTY
Kentucky	2007	Republican
Louisiana	2007	Democratic
Mississippi	2007	Republican
Delaware	2008	Democratic
Indiana	2008	Republican
Missouri	2008	Republican
Montana	2008	Democratic
New Hampshire	2008	Democratic
North Carolina	2008	Democratic
North Dakota	2008	Republican
Utah	2008	Republican
Vermont	2008	Republican
Washington	2008	Democratic
West Virginia	2008	Democratic
New Jersey	2009	Democratic
Virginia	2009	Democratic

Source: Adapted from data from the National Governors Association, "Governors of the United States, Commonwealths and Territories, 2007," www.nga.org/Files/pdf/BIOBOOK.pdf (accessed October 3, 2007).

general Jay Nixon. In Washington State, Democratic governor Christine Gregoire and Republican Dino Rossi are headed toward a rematch of a 2004 contest that Gregoire won by 129 votes out of 2.8 million cast.

Five other states elect their governors in odd-numbered years. Three of them— Kentucky, Louisiana, and Mississippi—elect their governors in odd-numbered years preceding presidential elections (2003, 2007, 2011, etc.). Because of the timing of those elections, the outcomes are often portrayed as political bellwethers and barometers of public opinion prior to the presidential elections.

In 2007, Republicans were favored to retain the governorship in Mississippi, where Republican incumbent Haley Barbour (a former chairman of the Republican National Committee) was favored against Democratic challenger John Arthur Eaves. The Republicans won in Louisiana, where U.S. representative Bobby Jindal maintained a big lead in polls through the summer of 2007 and was elected governor in October 2007. The Democrats, meanwhile, were waging a strong campaign in Kentucky, where former lieutenant governor Steven L. Beshear hoped to defeat Republican Gov. Ernie Fletcher, who is plagued by questions about his ethical behavior.

Virginia and New Jersey elect their governors in the odd-numbered years that follow presidential election years, and so serve as a barometer of public opinion about a presidential administration or the governing party in Congress. These states will hold their next elections for governor in 2009. In New Jersey, Democratic governor Jon Corzine is expected to seek reelection. Virginia is the only state in the nation that does not allow an incumbent governor to serve two consecutive four-year terms—so Democratic governor Tim Kaine, who was elected in 2005, cannot run for reelection in 2009. This quirk means that prospective candidates for Virginia governor can begin preparing campaigns for governor as soon as the previous governor's election is over.

Looking Ahead

There is much that we do not know about the 2008 election: namely who the presidential nominees will be and who ultimately will win the election that November. But it is clear that the 2008 election and subsequent elections will be influenced heavily by issues of national security and the ongoing war in Iraq. Most Democratic candidates for president have called for U.S. troops to be withdrawn from Iraq on a fixed timetable, while most Republican candidates have opposed a troop withdrawal.

Candidates for office in the 2008 election and in future elections will be grappling with other consequential issues. One is global climate change—and how the United States can reduce its use of harmful greenhouse gases and transition from a heavy dependence of foreign oil to greater use of renewable sources of energy. An upcoming wave of retirements from members of the baby boom generation—those born in the years immediately following World War II—will focus increased attention on improving the long-term financial health of the federal entitlement programs of Social Security and Medicare. In 2008 and beyond, political candidates will debate about how best to provide health insurance to the tens of millions of Americans who lack coverage and reduce the spiraling costs for those who do. There will be ongoing discussion about how to prevent illegal entry into the United States—and what to do with the millions of illegal immigrants who are already in this country.

There is widespread agreement about the issues that will dominate U.S. elections and political discourse. But it's not clear to what extent the two major political parties can come to agreement to solve any of them. Perhaps Democrats and Republicans will forge a consensus on one or more of these issues; perhaps they will not. Regardless of the extent to which federal policymakers will solve some of the nation's most pressing problems, these issues are likely to dominate the national agenda for many elections to come.

Notes

1. Charles E. Schumer, *Positively American* (New York: Rodale Inc., 2007), 74.
2. Jeannine Aversa and Ann Sanner, "Greenspan Faults Bush over Spending," The Associated Press, September 16, 2007, available at www.washingtonpost.com/wp-dyn/content/article/2007/09/15/AR2007091500858.html.
3. Remarks from Republican presidential debate at the University of South Carolina, Columbia, S.C., on May 15, 2007.
4. Federal Election Commission, *Federal Elections 2006,* available at www.fec.gov/pubrec/fe2006/federalelections2006.shtml.
5. This count includes Vermont, where liberal independent representative Bernard Sanders was elected to succeed another liberal independent, retiring senator James M. Jeffords. Though he is technically a political independent, Sanders aligns with the Democratic Party for organizational purposes.
6. www.fec.gov/press/press2007/partyfinal2006/20070307party.shtml.
7. Charles E. Schumer, *Positively American* (New York: Rodale Inc., 2007), 74.
8. http://kucinich.house.gov/News/DocumentSingle.aspx?DocumentID=73486.
9. Beth Fouhy, "Obama Says He's Agent of Change, Critiques Clinton," The Associated Press, September 3, 2007.
10. http://people-press.org/reports/pdf/353.pdf.
11. Bob Von Sternberg, "Giuliani Stops in Twin Cities for Coffee and Cash," *Star Tribune,* September 6, 2007, accessed at www.startribune.com/587/story/1405929.html.
12. http://pewforum.org/assets/files/religion-campaign08.pdf.
13. www.iowagop.net/straw.poll.asp.
14. http://gov.ca.gov/index.php?/press-release/5649/.
15. www.ny.gov/governor/press/0409071.html.
16. www.flgov.com/release/9011.
17. Rhodes Cook, *The Presidential Nominating Process: A Place for Us?* (Lanham, Md.: Rowman and Littlefield, 2004), 46.
18. www.house.gov/apps/list/press/mi12_levin/pr031407.html.
19. Marie Horrigan, "Blame Rove for Presidential Primary Mess, Says GOP Insider," CQPolitics.com, August 29, 2007, available at www.cqpolitics.com/2007/08/blame_rove_for_presidential_pr.html.

20. www.fec.gov/press/press2007/20070123limits.html.
21. www.cfinst.org/pr/prRelease.aspx?ReleaseID=155.
22. Available at www.hillaryclinton.com/news/release/view/?id=1234.
23. Available at http://www.fred08.com/FredCast/FredCastSummary.aspx.
24. From Sam Waterson's address delivered at the National Press Club, Washington, D.C., April 25, 2007.
25. www.mikebloomberg.com/en/issues/mike_discusses_2008_election.
26. Greg Giroux, "Third-Party Push: Hope vs. History," *CQ Weekly,* May 7, 2007, 1324.
27. www.cqpolitics.com/partyfundraising.html.
28. This compilation of forty-two Democrats first elected in 2006 includes three Democrats who had previously served in the House (Baron Hill of Indiana and Nick Lampson and Ciro D. Rodriguez of Texas).
29. www.fec.gov/press/press2007/20070814candidate/hseincrec2007.pdf.
30. www.fec.gov/press/press2007/20070814candidate/20070822can.shtml.
31. ABC *This Week* program, aired September 2, 2007.